THE
RISING LIFE

EVEN AMIDST THE CHAOS

Janet O. Ansah Oduro Bennett

There is no
force more
powerful than
a "WILL"
determined
to "RISE".

DEDICATION

To the glory of the Most High God.

The light, the voice, the presence, and the love that keep me going when the path feels too dark to walk.

To my son, Berimah:

You are my greatest gift from God and to mankind . Your presence in my life reminds me daily that love is worth every sacrifice. I rise so you can soar.

To every soul (of mankind) who has ever been broken, bruised, or buried by life's storms.

May you discover the quiet strength within you and the grace that never lets go. This is for your rising.

SPECIAL THANKS & ACKNOWLEDGEMENT

To my parents, Mr. William K. Owusu Ansah and Mrs. Felicia A. Owusu Ansah, thank you for teaching me about God and His love for me.

To my counsel, Akwasi A. Acheampong, Francis Kwesi Boachie, Chief Kwame Boateng Esq, Ebenezer Osei Bonsu, Robert Greenfield, Angelina Grimsley, HRH Mrs Mary Abena Agyepong, thank you for your sound counsel; it lifted me far beyond where I was.

To the Ghansah family, thank you for being a special source of provision and support.

To Dr. Emmanuel A. Affum of KNUST, Department of Computer Engineering, thank you for your guidance and support.

To Her Royal Highness, Nana Efua Dansoa Nkuma(I) (Oheneyere Gifty Anti), Dr. Cindy Trimm of The Trimm Ministry and Dr. Myron Golden (Public Speaker) for your inspiration and influence on my work.

To Will and Peg Balzer, Charles Williamson, Nathaniel Wysong, and Janell Bourn, thank you for your kindness and unwavering support.

To my siblings, cousins, nephews, nieces, grandchildren, and great-grandchildren, thank you for your love, encouragement, and support.

To my family and friends across the globe, thank you for the unmatched love and encouragement you continue to pour into my ministry.

To my publishing team, NY book publishers, for an awesome work.

FOREWORD

We have had the privilege of watching the author's life unfold—not from a safe distance, but up close, through the quiet triumphs and the unspoken tears. We have known the author not only as a voice of wisdom but as a living example of resilience. Privileged to have seen her wrestle with seasons of trials and tribulations that would have brought even the strongest to their knees, and yet somehow, she rose triumphant. Not because the road was easy, but because her spirit refused defeat. Having lived a greater number of years in Africa, Jane grew up in Ghana, where the West is viewed as the place to be, the only place where dreams highly came true; life would later carry her across oceans to the United States, where new dreams awaited, along with new challenges that would test the very core of her strength. And, alas, she dreamed, and her dream came to life, which is now her reality. Author of: "The Rising Life, Even Amidst the Chaos". What makes The Rising Life, Even Amidst the Chaos so profound is that it is not theory—it is a testimony. The words in these pages are not the product of a comfortable life, but of one that has known upheaval, loss, reinvention, and the courage to begin again. They are written by someone who stood in the middle of storms that threatened to break her, but emerged steadfast and stronger. This is not simply a book—it is a living testament borne from nights of unanswered questions, from moments when the future seemed uncertain, and from a heart that chose life, determination, endurance, and hope when despair was the easier choice. What gives this work its uniqueness is that it carries the fingerprints of authenticity. The author does not speak from a pedestal, but from the very ground where she, too, has struggled. They offer no false promises, only the real possibility of renewal that comes when you shift your perspective, embrace the lessons hidden in the pain, and dare to believe that even in chaos, life can still be beautiful. The beauty of this book is that it speaks to the universal human journey—whether your storm is individual or family, penury or profligacy, physical, or spiritual, it meets you where you are, in the heart of your entropy, and reminds you that there is still life, still desire and hope, still purpose waiting to be claimed. Reading these pages feels like sitting with a trusted friend who tells you, "I know it hurts, but you are stronger than you think." It is both a mirror, showing you where you are, and a compass, guiding you toward where you can go. Through every chapter, you will feel the heartbeat of a person who has carried their roots proudly, who has learned from two worlds, and who now offers these lessons to you—not as a distant advisor, but as a trusted friend who has walked this path. Because even though the West is portrayed to be the place of all possibilities, she embraces her noble roots and fashioned her journey forward on the principles woven in her being by the struggles, perseverance, and triumphs in her original homeland of Africa. If you are holding this book, it is no coincidence. You were meant to find it at this moment in your journey. Let it remind you that the storms may be loud, but they will not last forever. It simply offers new perspectives, cleansing and renewal, a realignment of your axis, and a shift in the direction of your compass. Let it inspire you to rise, not when the sky clears, but right here, where the winds are loud and the waves are high, in the middle of it all. Because as the author's journey shows us, you are not defined by the chaos—you are defined by your rising.

HRH, Daasebre Okatakyie Nana Adarkwa Boakye Yiadom I [Dwantuahene, Nsawam Adoagyiri, Ghana/USA] Mr. I. D. Appiasam [Customer Experience Professional, SSB, Hospitality Industry, USA]

Contents

["The LORD is my Shepherd, I will lack nothing." Psa 23:1 Rcv]
["Blessed is everyone who fears the LORD, who walks in His ways." Psa 128:1]

INTRODUCTION

THE RISING LIFE, EVEN AMIDST THE CHAOS

My early life in Africa was full of color, tradition, excitement, and a strong sense of community. But it was also marked by unspoken pain, silent sacrifices, and the quiet strength of a young girl seemingly carrying more than her share of life's weight through its unpredictable turns.

Later, I found myself as an immigrant in the United States of America, a new land, a new beginning, and an entirely new set of challenges. I was now a mother, raising my beloved son, while navigating unfamiliar systems, balancing work and faith, and silently wrestling with loss, rejection, and the deep longing to feel whole.

There were days I questioned everything—days when I smiled in public but cried behind closed doors, days when my prayers felt like whispers lost in the boisterous wind. Yet even in those moments, something within me refused to let go. A still, small voice kept reminding me: You are not forgotten. You are loved.

That voice—God's presence—became my anchor.

This book, *The Rising Life, Even Amidst the Chaos,* is the story of how I learned to rise again, not because life became easier, but because I began to see it differently. I came to understand that chaos doesn't always mean defeat. Sometimes, it's a holy disruption—a divine invitation to rediscover who you truly are beneath the noise, beneath the pain, beneath the labels.

Through each chapter, I share not only my journey but also the wisdom gathered along the way: the courage to face the truth, the healing found in it, the grace to forgive, and the strength to dream and hope again. You will find my faith woven throughout these pages, because it was faith that carried me when my own strength had run out.

This book is for anyone who has ever felt caught between who they used to be and who they are becoming. It is for the weary, the seekers, the fathers and mothers, the immigrants, the overcomers, and those still wandering in what I call "the nowhere." It is both a reflection of my journey and a message of hope to all who find themselves lost in the clattering of life. It is a guide for the heart, a mirror for the soul, and a reminder that even in the midst of confusion and chasm, life still rises.

If you're holding this book, I believe you're ready for something deeper, for clarity, renewal, and a fresh perspective. I invite you to journey with me, to reflect, and to rise, not in perfection, but in purpose.

Welcome to *The Rising Life.*

THE RISING LIFE, EVEN AMIDST THE CHAOS

CHAPTER ONE

❖ REDIFINING THE ODDS TO WORK IN YOUR FAVOR :

The odds were never meant to define you — they were meant to reveal you. Like the first life of a seed, mankind has been endowed with limitless possibilities of redefining every and any situation in our favor. This means to be and succeed in abundance is our birthright from creation. We have been blessed beyond human comprehension to be fruitful and multiply in every undertaking we pursue and to replenish this earth with our whole existence, our activities, and to have dominion over everything on earth and in all areas of our lives. Unfortunately, on our part, this command has been met with some resistance through unbelief, doubt, and unwillingness to receive, costing mankind in a way that is unthinkable. [Gen 1:28]

[It is not what is contained in a book that will enlighten or illumine me, but how I accept, receive, and apply the knowledge or principles found in it that makes all the difference- Unknown.]

["But be ye doers of the word, and not hearers only, deceiving your own selves." James 1: 22 KJV]

["For it is God which worketh in you both to will and to do of His good pleasure." Phil 2:13 KJV]

"~Only the antifragile is capable of ruling, thriving in abundance, and living their best life-" Unknown

When you know who you are — spiritually, mentally, emotionally and physically— the odds lose power. Identity shifts the equation. Identity breaks assumptions. Identity is the foundation that tells the world who you truly are unapologetically.

As an immigrant from Ghana, W/Africa, born as the first of five children to my parents, my early years were shaped by movement through mainly three influential cities in Africa: The vibrant and royal streets of Kumasi, the quiet hills of Kibi, and the bustling heartbeat of Accra, the nation's capital. Each of these unique places left an imprint on my soul—cultivating a deep sense of resilience, identity, and adaptability. These culturally rich and diverse environments helped shape my character, instilling in me a quiet strength and a deep appreciation for the richness of life's complexities.

Now living in the United States with my son, I continue to pursue excellence in both my academic and professional life, and *[I am currently a graduate student at Georgia State University and serving in a prominent role at a prestigious real estate firm in downtown Atlanta, Georgia].*

My journey has not been without struggle. I have wrestled through seasons of loss, cultural transition, and emotional pain. At a point, I found myself in a place of deep darkness and despair, where I could no longer see a way forward. But it was precisely in that place that I had a divine touch and I have not been the same on a deeper level again. Here is where I began to rise—learning how to break free from the shadows of brokenness, expectations of who I should be and society's dictates, and reaching deep within myself to connect to my inner spirit and ultimately stepping boldly into the light of my purpose.

My journey has been one of unlearning, relearning, becoming and being. It is a testament to what can happen when a person refuses to give up, even when every reason to quit surrounds them. Fueled by faith, desire, and an unshakable inner strength, I figured out ways to transform my pain into purpose and now use my voice to uplift others.

There is a moment in every person's life's journey when you rise above just what you see, hear and feel physically, *[the noise, the emotion, the confusion, and the immediate facts]* — and you begin to see from a higher plane. This is not denial,

4

and it is not avoidance. It is **spiritual intelligence**. It is the ability to step out of survival mode and step into divine perspective.   When you perceive from a higher perspective, you stop reacting to what is happening to and around you and start discerning what is unfolding before you and for you. You begin to recognize patterns, lessons, and spiritual alignments.   You no longer see the moment in isolation — you see it as part of a much larger divine design.This shift turns chaos into clarity.

As I relive my life from the remaining pieces, the only obvious things left for me that have been consistently recurring are the insights and altitudes gained, visions seen, lessons learned, and observations made through the lens of life itself. Through these experiences, I was reminded that we, as a people, don't have to wait for the storm to pass before we begin to move forward again.   From a higher vantage point, my situation changed shape. Obstacles shrank. Options multiplied. And the same storm that once threatened me became the wind that lifted me to where I find myself today. I began to benefit not by changing the situation, but by changing my position.

We must *learn to dance in the rain, enjoy the sunshine and shine bright in the night as luminaries.* Through the insights shared in this book, readers are reminded that their past does not define them and that renewal and fulfillment of purpose are always available and possible. And that success is within reach if only they're willing and believe.

CHAPTER TWO

❖ THE COMEBACK (ASCENDING)

["For I returned, and saw under the sun, that the race is not to the swift, nor the battle to the strong, nor yet bread to the wise, nor yet riches to men of understanding, nor yet favor to men of skill; but time and chance happens to them all." Eccles 9:11]

★ Wisdom Emerges When You Rise Above Your Situation

Witnessing what is happening before you cannot be denied, but how you perceive it determines whether you are always going to have an accurate interpretation of the situation or not. When you elevate your perspective, your spirit leads, your mind becomes calm, your soul becomes centered and your inner being becomes aligned with the divine. This creates spiritual stability — the ability to see clearly even when the environment is still in chaos.

Everyone might have, at some stage of their life, seen the destruction of what they had built and established, without a warning. And I am not an exception. I have seen it happen in real life and even worse, in the darkest moments of my life. Yet nothing discouraged me from desiring to attain the heights I had envisioned and live the life I saw myself living. I learned to mind my business and work toward the vision with determination, focus and perseverance.

["Mind your business, crush your goals, and make moves in silence. You don't need an audience to achieve greatness..." Morgan Richard Oliver]

Understanding that a higher perspective turns pain into power, what once felt like loss became redirection. What once looked like failure became refinement. What once seemed like a setback became preparation. From a higher perspective, the

6

purpose of my struggle became visible. Now I move with insight, not instinct. Higher perception allows me to make decisions from vision, not fear, from wisdom, not impulse, and from alignment, not exhaustion. This thus became my spiritual advantage as a person who had a paradigm shift— the ability to walk in clarity.

You may have numerous reasons to back out and give up on life when you think your dreams are never going to be realized. You may have experienced some difficulties, disappointments, and setbacks, which may have taken the excitement out of you and ultimately knocked you down. Know this, that's all part of the process and journey to a fulfilling and successful life. Get back up again, knowing that God did not bring you this far just to leave you. No, that's not His hallmark! Don't ever settle for mediocracy, for it can get you stuck for the rest of your life.

It is imperative to remember that you were created for greatness by your Creator. And your Maker intends to transform you and your name into something great. Our Creator is into greatness and great names. Abraham was given the promise that he would be made great and his name and his descendants would be great, if Abraham would just believe, and he did believe in God, and it was counted to him as righteousness.

[*"And I will make of thee a great nation, and I will bless thee, and make thy name great; and thou shalt be a blessing: ..and in thee shall all families of the earth be blessed." Gen12:2-3 KJV*]

There is something within you that causes you to stand out among the crowd, and that refuses to back down when everything around comes crashing down. You have something that nobody else has or can do. You have been placed here on earth for such a time as this, because a seed has been planted within you that will cause you to make and leave a lasting legacy wherever you are planted, and an influence on whoever and whatever you come into contact with.

People who lack understanding of who you are may see your potential and deem it necessary to distract you from your assignment; you don't have to let them. Don't let failures convince you to give up. Don't let delays and detours cause you to be discouraged, and certainly don't allow yourself to lose hope and faith by believing the lies you may tell yourself. You are not weak. You are not lacking in anything. You are very powerful and full of abilities to become who you are meant to be, to do anything you are enabled to do, and to overcome any obstacles in your life's journey.

["I am able to do all things through Christ who strengthens me!" Phil 4:13]

Just keep staying committed, consistent, persistent, confident and focused on your assignment, being your best in executing the service to mankind, and standing firm in your values and principles of your purpose, and see the reward of open gates, doors, and windows of opportunities by the Most High Himself. Opportunities that you could never have imagined or would have been able to create by yourself. Your ability to see the reward becomes a reality of supernatural peace & strategic momentum. When you see from above, you operate with a calm spirit, a renewed mind, a grounded soul, and a focused body.
This integration unlocks your ability to benefit from every experience, even the ones meant to break you.

["But as it is written: Eye hath not seen, nor ear heard, neither have entered into the heart of man the things which God hath prepared for them that love Him." 1 Cor 2:9]

8

Indeed, God has something more rewarding for you than you ever imagined. Stay connected to the source, ABBA.

["I know your works. Behold, I have set before you an open door, and no man can shut it. For you have a little strength, and have kept My Word, and have not denied My name." Rev 3:8 Rcv]

Life feels like an uphill battle, especially when the odds seem stacked against you as you ascend into the heights of your life.

Your Life is essentially your ascendancy into a higher calling through ordained experiences and activities that lead to the uncovering of your higher purpose. And this life has an interesting way of sharing its sense of humor when it comes to opening up the hidden secrets and treasures of life, the rewards, to mankind, completely out of our consideration, making life a mystery yet to be discovered as we journey through it.

["But the path of the just(righteous) is like the light of dawn; which shines brighter and brighter until (it reaches its full strength and glory in) the perfect(full) day." Prov 4:18 AMP]

CHAPTER THREE

❖ CHOICES ARE FOR LIFE

["I call heaven and earth to record this day against you that I have set before you life and death, blessing and cursing. Therefore, (I admonish you to) choose life, so that you and your seed will live" ... Deut 30: 19.KJV]

This is your comeback, your destiny. What choice have you made lately?

[*"Therefore, choose life, so that you and your seed will live." 30:19b. *]

Choices are the gatekeepers of destiny. A choice is more than an action; it is a spiritual agreement. Every choice opens a door or closes one. Every choice creates alignment or misalignment. Every choice draws you closer to your desired results or deeper into undesired cycles. When you choose with intention, you participate in shaping your destiny rather than drifting through it.

To live is a choice we make, consciously or unconsciously, every day of our lives. Choices are changes and the only thing constant in life is change; therefore, choices are constant changes we make throughout our lifetime. To have life is to walk in the way of the truth. That is to live according to the purpose of your existence by going through set experiences that are able to make you into the person who becomes capable in every situation and fully equipped for every good work.

["Life is about falling, and living is about rising up from the fall". Unknown]

Life responds to the choices you make. Life is not passive — it reacts, reflects, and rearranges itself around your choices and decisions. When you choose healing, life brings opportunities to heal. When you choose growth, life stretches your potential. When you choose truth, life reveals clarity and when you choose purpose, life unveils pathways. You are not at the mercy of circumstances; you are in partnership with the future you create.

Some scholars have defined life by abbreviating the word L.I.F.E as Living in Freedom Eternally. This concept has added a new perspective to the understanding of Life, bringing us to the concept of eternal life, which is the promised life of all believers in Christ, a teaching concerning the kingdom of heaven in scripture. Choices become cycles, and cycles become lifestyles, a way of life and thus become a culture. Repeated choices form patterns. Patterns form habits. Habits form cycles. And cycles, whether healthy or destructive, eventually become lifestyles, and a way of life—culture. This is why conscious choice-making is essential — it determines whether you are living in bondage or living in freedom.

Life requires living; freedom is the ability to make decisions and choices from within oneself, without a maximum influence of external forces. Freedom is not for some other time; it is for the life we are living in the present. Eternity is the forever present, irrespective of the past or the future and it is within us.

["He has made everything beautiful in its time: also, He has put eternity into their heart, ..." Eccles 3: 11]

Whether it is in your spiritual life, family life, career and business, personal growth, or financial stability, overcoming obstacles requires a mindset (strategic action), a believing heart(faith), and a relentless determination (perseverance).

How are you able to overcome every situation in life? By believing possibilities!

The good news? Just as we believe that God created mankind from the dust of the ground, you have been empowered with talent and ability to create from your situation and turn things around in your favor for good, only if you believe. The power to overcome and thrive is embedded in your DNA! You have the ability to turn adversity into opportunity, challenges into stepping stones, tests into testimonies, poverty into prosperity, and setbacks into comebacks. This can result in your living in abundance with no limits and no regrets, only gratitude and joy.

It is often said that everything you've been looking for and are not able to find it where you are now is on the other side of the unknown, and therefore requires you to make a turn when necessary. Even what you feel has its opposite and it can be in the form of energy, and therefore, if we endeavor to take a leap of faith forward to the other side, we can be sure to find everything, every result, and every answer we are seeking.

["But without faith it is impossible to [walk with God and] please Him, for whoever comes [near] to God must [necessarily] believe that God exists and that He rewards those who [earnestly and diligently] seek Him." Heb 11:6 AMP]

["And thine ears shall hear a word behind thee, saying, "This is the way; walk ye in it," when ye turn to the right hand and when ye turn to the left." Isaiah 30:21 KJV]

[And He said unto them, "Cast the net on the right side of the boat, and you shall find." They cast, therefore, and now they

were not able to draw it in for the multitude of fishes." John 21:6 RcV]

This is how you can flip the odds, being willing to make the necessary adjustments through choices to obtain the desired outcome and thrive in abundance in your field of expertise while doing life, ruling, reigning, and dominating the best of life even in the midst of the obstreperous and disarray. Here, the required virtue is obedience.

Your future waits on the choices you make today. Where you stand tomorrow is shaped by the decisions you make today. Your future is not a mystery — it is a mirror. It reflects the strength, clarity, and courage of today's choices. Even one intentional choice can shift the entire trajectory of your life. Life honors those who choose with purpose. That is when your choices align with who you are, who God created you to be, and who you are becoming and being. Then life begins to cooperate with your identity, your purpose, and your destiny. Your choices are your everyday declarations: "I choose life. I choose progress and prosperity. I choose healing and happiness. I choose in freedom the future that is meant for me."

CHAPTER FOUR

❖ REFRAME CHALLENGES AS OPPORTUNITIES

Many people view obstacles as roadblocks and immediately become discouraged about the situation and their ability to change their perspective on it; however, the most successful individuals recognize them as hidden opportunities. Instead of seeing obstacles, they see opportunities, and instead of focusing on problems, they focus on possibilities. Instead of focusing on what's going wrong, you can initiate a dialogue within yourself by asking yourself questions that may also enable you to find solutions and still keep your inner joy intact.

● PRACTICAL TECHNIQUES FOR REDEFINING CHALLENGES

★ What can I learn from this situation?

★ How can this challenge make me a stronger and better person?

★ What is the hidden opportunity here? In what ways can I derive effective solutions from and for this situation efficiently?

★ What was my role in this situation, a contributor and or as part of the solution? Do I recognize my direct or indirect influence on this situation/ Am I willing to accept responsibility, honest accountability, and assist in finding solutions?

Most of the time in situations and likely conflicts, people are not able or willing to have the difficult conversations with themselves first to accept responsibility and become accountable. This is mainly the reason most people are unable to have difficult dialogues within their relationships, because they are not at peace with themselves.

When you are in touch with the peace of God within your heart, you shift your perspective and obtain a new and better understanding of your situation, with the knowledge that there is something to gain at the end of it all. You gain a higher perspective and begin to see solutions instead of challenges, abundance instead of lack or limitations. Always remember, in every message, there was a mess before the dawn of the age, and the message always brings in the light. The message is expected to enlighten and bring liberation. Also, always remember that from the pattern presented from the beginning of creation, disruption always follows great intention, but the truth, through light, is always emerging victorious in the end.

Perceptions determine perspectives. How you perceive things, including yourself and others, defines your perspective of yourself and others. With the right perception, perspective, and mindset, you become unstoppable and limitless in achieving success and manifesting abundance in all areas of your life. And with the right amount of enlightenment of your mind, you acquire the best perspective of virtually everything in life. The virtue required here is open mindedness for enlightenment.

Reframing challenges as opportunities is a powerful mindset shift that can transform how you experience life. The following are some benefits:

★ Encourages Growth and Learning – Challenges often carry lessons. Seeing them as opportunities helps you develop resilience, adaptability, and new skills.

★ Boosts Problem-Solving – Instead of getting stuck on the problem, you train your mind to look for creative solutions and possibilities.

★ Strengthens Resilience – You bounce back quicker when setbacks are viewed as stepping stones rather than roadblocks.

★ Reduces Stress and Anxiety – Challenges feel less overwhelming when framed as opportunities for improvement, exploration, or self-discovery.

★ Builds Confidence – Each time you overcome a reframed challenge, your belief in your ability to handle adversity grows.

★ Inspires Optimism – You cultivate a positive outlook, making it easier to stay motivated and hopeful in difficult times.

★ Opens New Doors – Opportunities often hide within obstacles. Reframing helps you notice paths and connections you might have missed.

★ Deepens Purpose and Meaning – Challenges often clarify your values and priorities, helping you live with greater intention.

Life has a way of presenting us with moments that test our strength. At times, these moments may feel unbearable—like a heavy weight pressing down, leaving us uncertain of how to move forward. Challenges come in many forms: loss, disappointment, setbacks, or unexpected changes. Yet, within every challenge lies a hidden seed of opportunity, waiting to be recognized and nurtured.

When we shift our perspective, something remarkable happens. A difficulty that once seemed like an immovable burden begins to transform into a stepping stone. What looked like a wall reveals itself as a doorway. Reframing challenges as opportunities doesn't erase the pain or remove the struggle, but it does reshape how we walk through them. Instead of being defined by obstacles, we become shaped by the growth they call forth from us.

Every challenge is an invitation to step outside of what is comfortable and discover new dimensions of ourselves. Hardship stretches us in ways comfort never could. It teaches us resilience, the ability to stand up again after being knocked down. It cultivates creativity, pushing us to find solutions we never would have imagined otherwise. It deepens our courage, urging us to trust that beyond every obstacle lies a possibility waiting to be revealed.

Failures, too, can be reframed. When seen through the lens of opportunity, failure is no longer final—it becomes feedback, a teacher pointing us toward new directions and better ways. Detours that once felt like delays can eventually be understood as redirections, guiding us to places we might not have reached if life had gone exactly as we planned.

This shift in mindset opens the door to hope, confidence, and purpose. It allows us to see that life is not simply happening to us—it is happening for us. Every trial carries within it the potential for transformation, shaping us into who we are meant to become.

When we choose to reframe challenges as opportunities, we move from a posture of defeat to one of empowerment. We begin to trust the process, even when it is difficult, and to trust ourselves more deeply. Pain becomes a source of power. Struggle becomes the soil from which destiny grows.

The truth is simple yet profound: every challenge carries a gift. It may not be obvious in the moment, but when we lean into the lessons it offers, we discover that the very experiences meant to break us can also be the ones that build us into who we are destined to be.

CHAPTER FIVE

❖ **DEVELOP AN UNSTOPPABLE GROWTH MINDSET**

Success isn't about luck—it's about mindset. A growth mindset involves believing that you can improve through learning, unlearning, relearning, and adapting regardless of the circumstances or challenges. Achieving excellence is not cheap; it requires discipline, dedication, and willingness. While your starting point is important for your growth and success, they are just part of the bigger picture. A growth mindset is a determining factor and can be defined as the belief that abilities and intelligence can be developed through effort, learning, and persistence. This mindset can significantly impact your career prospects and business success in every area of your life. It reflects the intrinsic ability to sustain the idea of life itself.

So, your attitude, environment, and surroundings are crucial for your growth, success, and abundance. Recognizing that your attitude influences your altitude, your environment and surroundings also shape your alignment, and all these elements impact your mindset. This is a universal principle that isn't tied to religion or a set of imaginary rules to be applied but is fundamentally about relationships—your relationship first with God, then with yourself, and finally with others.

Nature requires growth and maturity to manifest abundance, and in principle, abundance is accelerated growth and dominion. With a growth mindset as your foundation, every situation becomes an opportunity for you to grow and elevate to the next level of your life. You become a person who does not pivot at the sight of adversity, but faces the turbulence head-on until the flight reaches a safe place for touchdown.

- **PRACTICAL TECHNIQUES FOR PERSONAL, AND PROFESSIONAL GROWTH**

  ★ Suggested Mindset for Career Prospects;

  Pursue continuous Learning and skill development at all levels. You're more likely to seek out opportunities to improve your skills (e.g., taking courses, asking for feedback, learning from failure). This makes you more adaptable to new technologies and job market demands.

  ★ Resilience in the Face of Setbacks

  Instead of giving up when you fail, you treat challenges as learning opportunities.

  This persistence is crucial in competitive job markets or when facing rejection.

  ★ Better Performance Reviews and Promotions

  Employers value employees who are proactive about growth.

  You're seen as coachable, which is attractive for leadership development.

  ★ Enhanced Networking and Collaboration

  You tend to value learning from others, which fosters stronger personal and professional relationships and partnerships.

Develop a Growth Mindset because how you think determines how you grow, and learn to embrace challenges as opportunities to improve, not as threats to your competence. Continue to stay curious, ask questions, and be open to feedback. View failure as data: Initiate analysis on feedback.

Ask: What did it teach me? How can I adjust? How can I improve and grow in this way? Embrace failure as feedback. Understand that there are two sides to every person, thing, and situation, and what we may perceive as failure is actually a form of response being communicated to us for adjustment, clarity,   and accountability. The virtue here is willingness/willpower.

★ Surround yourself with people who inspire and challenge you to become better as a person and in everything you do and say.   Build strategic partnerships, connections, and relationships. Your circle determines your tribe. Your network also significantly influences your net worth. Understanding that your wealth encompasses not just the amount of money you have, but also the time you have to spend with your family and friends, your physical health, and your social connections is crucial.

★ Continuously seek new skills and knowledge to elevate your expertise and aspire to become the next big command in your circle of expertise. Venture into new terrains and take calculated risks in spite of the uncertainty. Knowing that posterity rewards the **bold** and **daring.**

★ Be willing to share your knowledge and experiences to help others navigate and grow in life. This practice has the potential of opening unexpected opportunities for you. Sharing has everything to do with gratitude and emphasizes the importance of sharing our knowledge, experience, and wisdom through our work with others. *"Feeling gratitude and not expressing it is like wrapping a present   and not giving it out ".* **William Arthur Ward**

★ Elevate your thinking and thought processes, but do not think too highly of yourself as being better than others. Understand that we're all excellent in our respective individual capacities; the only difference is access and opportunities. Never compare yourself with others because comparison is a thief of joy. Knowing that we have all been called to a unique and different assignment, to an aspect of the building.

("...but they, measuring themselves with themselves, and comparing themselves among themselves, are not wise." ... 2 Cor 10:12-13. RcV)

("For I say, through the grace given to me, to everyone among you, not to think more highly of himself than he ought to think, but to think so as to be sober-minded, as God has apportioned to each a measure of faith." Rom 12:3 RCv)

★ Be thankful for every situation whether 'good' or 'bad', because opportunities always come wrapped up as challenges. Gratitude expresses appreciation and thankfulness, always highlighting its positive impact on life and relationships.

"Gratitude is the fairest blossom which springs from within the soul ". **Henry Ward Beecher.**

In showing our gratitude, we express our joy in its purest and highest form. Experiencing joy is a natural manifestation of gratitude. *"Joy is the simplest form of gratitude".* Karl Barth.

CHAPTER SIX

❖ **TAKE CALCULATED RISK- NEVER ENTERTAIN FEAR**

While risk involves uncertainty, it's often the key to unlocking your full potential. Risk-taking is important because it drives personal growth, innovation, and progress. Without stepping out of your comfort zone, it's hard to reach new opportunities or achieve significant success. Its benefits include personal growth, where taking risks challenges you to adapt, learn, and build resilience. Even if the outcome isn't what you hoped for, you gain valuable experience. And also, professional growth, either corporately or in an individual business.

New potential possibilities in which many great opportunities lie beyond the familiar are often overlooked. Whether it's a new job, a business venture, or a life decision, taking a calculated risk can open doors you never expected. Increased confidence comes from each time you take a risk and either survive or succeed, building trust in your ability to handle uncertainty and making decisions. Innovation and creativity show that risk-taking is the foundation of progress. Trying something new often leads to fresh ideas and breakthroughs.

Avoiding regret by playing it safe all the time can lead to lingering "what if" regrets later in life. Taking a chance helps you live more fully and free of doubts. To improve your chances, you must be willing to take risks, be daring, and brave. However, successful risk-taking isn't about being reckless; it's about being strategic in your moves.

A strategic move in risk management involves making calculated decisions that help a person anticipate, mitigate, or leverage risks to achieve their objectives. These moves are often proactive rather than reactive and align with the person's overall strategy. Taking calculated risks enhances resilience and long-term sustainability, protects brand reputation, and helps maintain regulatory compliance, and also improves your confidence and that of your stakeholders.

- **PRACTICAL RISK-TAKING TECHNIQUES TO EMPLOY:**

  ★ Establish your intentions through your imaginations, desires, thoughts, and actions. Your imagination is your link to the infinite source of existence and possibilities of the divine, which has the potential of revealing the creator within you. Desires unveil the true essence of your being; they are beliefs that shape your reality through your thoughts and actions.   *["For as he thinketh in his heart, so is he:.. Prov 23:7a KJV]*

★ Do your research before making big decisions. Research is a form of preparation and shows you mean business; research, like mining, will provide you with the basic ground, the necessary information, and relevant knowledge to assist you with the decision-making process. It is the foundation for creation. Information enlightens and clarifies your thought process, enabling you to access your best ideas that are hidden within you all along. Therefore, seek knowledge through reading, listening, analyzing, and comprehending ideas.   *["The beginning of wisdom is this: Get wisdom; and in all your getting, get understanding."   Prov 4:7.   KJV]*

★ Weigh the potential benefits of the thoughts, ideas and actions against the possible setbacks. If the benefits outweigh the challenges, take that opportunity, step forward and make the move. Never procrastinate or undermine the opportunity presented before you, and know that tomorrow is never guaranteed. Therefore, take the chance today to fulfill the day's purpose. Here, time is essential, remembering that time is a limited resource in the life of man on earth.

★ Take action despite uncertainty, because waiting for the "perfect" time is an illusion. Knowing that faith is taking that first step without seeing the next, and yet believing that there is a way forward. Faith affords you the ability to hear and to move. Always remember that. *["Whether you turn to the right or to the left, your ears will hear a voice behind you saying, "This is the way; walk in it."... Isaiah 30:21. KJV]*

★ Do the thing you're most uncomfortable with and that really scares you. I am referring to facing your greatest fear. I am talking about the brilliant idea that came to mind while you were meditating this morning, or the idea about a business niche when you were doing something you liked to do so much. Ideas that seem impossible to you must be in your radar for consideration. This is where your breakthrough comes from. *["Every mountain and hill will be made level and every valley will be brought high." Isaiah 40:4]*

★ **Ways to unlock opportunities through skills specialization**

Skills specialization in a particular skill-set can set you apart in a competitive job market. And identifying niche areas within your industry where demand is high but expertise is low or scarce allows you to position yourself as a valuable asset. For instance, professionals in digital or conventional marketing could focus on data-driven strategies, while those specialized in information technology (IT) might specialize in data analytics, data mining, cybersecurity, AI, and cloud infrastructure or data machine learning. Developing expertise through certifications, workshops, and real-world experience ensures your skills remain relevant and in demand.

Once you've honed your specialization, you need a specific product or service to leverage it to create a personal brand. Then you can share insights, publish articles, or present at industry events to establish yourself and your brand as an authority in your field. These efforts not only boost your personal and professional reputation but also attract opportunities that align with your personal and professional values, objectives and interests. Focused specialization combined with strategic self-development, industry-specific training, brand promotion, and cross-industry partnerships can significantly accelerate your career growth.

★ The Purpose and Benefits of Calculated Risk

Taking calculated risks is not reckless living—it is courage guided by wisdom, intuition reinforced by preparation, and faith aligned with action. Life expands or contracts in proportion to the risks we are willing to take. Growth rarely happens inside the comfort zone; it happens at the edges—where uncertainty meets opportunity, where discomfort becomes a doorway, and where bold choices shape destiny.   Calculated risks serve a higher purpose to break limitations, expand identity, and position you for opportunities that cannot be accessed through safety alone. You take risks not for the thrill, but for elevation – becoming more capable, confident, and resilient, with alignment – thus walking closer to your calling and deeper purpose, and breakthrough – stepping into the stages of life meant for you. Where there is no risk, there is no transformation.

What Makes a Risk "Calculated"? A calculated risk is a strategic decision, not an impulsive one. It combines: **Information** — What you know and identify as facts, possibilities, and potential outcomes.   **Insight** — What experience has taught you and the wisdom you have drawn from past victories and failures. **Intuition** — What your inner spirit discerns and what makes you lean into that inner knowing—where peace, conviction, and clarity live. **Intention** — Why you're doing what you are doing and whether your motives are aligned with growth, purpose, and long-term vision. When these four align, risk becomes a path—not a gamble.

The personal side of calculated risk often requires saying "yes" to the unfamiliar and "no" to what is comfortable, familiar, but limiting. *Some scenarios may include, choosing healing over repeating old cycles, leaving environments that shrink your identity, setting boundaries where none existed before, starting fresh after loss, trauma, or transition, and pursuing personal dreams despite fear or doubt.* These choices are not easy—but they create a new self, one aligned with freedom, identity, and destiny. Every healed version of yourself is the result of a risk taken.

The professional side of calculated risk *often requires applying for a role you're not 100% "ready" for, launching a business or creative project, investing in your education or skill set, networking and being visible,*
asking for promotions, raises, or new responsibilities, and switching industries or careers. Great careers are often built on decisions that require courage at the beginning. People who advance are not the most talented—they're the ones willing to take strategic risks consistently.

Calculated risks strengthen you and create internal expansion including *greater confidence*— where you learn that you can handle uncertainty and challenge. *Increased resilience*— where you grow stronger emotionally and mentally. *Heightened clarity*— where you learn what you want, what you don't want, and who you are. *Elevated opportunities*— where growth opens doors that comfort zones keep locked. *Deeper spiritual alignment*— where stepping out in courage often unlocks destiny. You become bolder, wiser, and more aligned with your calling.

The spiritual dimension indicates that many breakthroughs require faith-based courage. The spirit often leads you into places your comfort zone would never walk. Calculated risks become a partnership with divine timing, inner wisdom, higher purpose, and destiny unfolding. It is in those decisive moments—when you trust beyond what you can see—that transformation happens.

The art of measuring risks requires you to ask yourself, *What is the best possible outcome? What is the worst possible outcome? What is the cost of not taking the risk?*

Can I prepare, plan, or build skills to reduce uncertainty?

The last question is where growth happens— risk becomes manageable when your preparation rises.

The cost of playing it safe in an effort to avoid risk often leads to missed opportunities, delayed purpose, emotional stagnation, unfulfilled potential, and regret for what could have been comfort or feels safe, but it has a high price—*your destiny remains dormant.* The reward of choosing courage is enormous. Every bold, calculated decision plants seeds of your future. Taking risks does not guarantee immediate success—but it guarantees constant learning, continuous expansion, increased momentum, definite identity shift, and access to new possibilities. Success is not the outcome of certainty—it is the outcome of courage.

["For I know the plans I have for you," declares the LORD, "plans to prosper you and not to harm you, plans to give you hope and a future." Jer 29:11 NKJV]

CHAPTER SEVEN

❖ LEVERAGE THE POWER OF NETWORKING

("And the LORD God said, it is not good for the man to be alone; I will make him a helper as his counterpart...". Gen 2:18.   RCv)

No one succeeds in isolation. Your ability to build relationships can be your greatest and most valuable asset. Your life is your business, and business is simply serving people with their needs based on your skills and abilities. Without people, there is no us, and therefore no business. So, learn to notice and appreciate people. Because your life isn't just about you; it's about others also. You control how you interact with others, how much time you spend with them, how much information you share, and how much influence you have by treating people like they are essential to your livelihood, because they actually are. Instead of treating people like they're an inconvenience, treat them like your own self, and watch how the game changes in your favor. God, in His infinite wisdom and sovereignty, has given us all the gifts and talents we need to build and grow in every area of our lives; but He ensured we will only be fruitful and multiply when we are built up together with others.

Never assume you're self-sufficient; that conflicts with the principles of fruitfulness, multiplication, replenishing, abundance, and domination. As human beings, we are created to depend first on God, our Creator, and on one another. Similarly, a seed needs the earth to be fruitful; the earth requires water, sunlight, and other nutrients to be fertile enough for the seed. For a tree, the roots need the stem to support them, the stem needs the roots for stability, the branches need the stem to grow and stabilize, the fruits and leaves rely on the branches for growth and structure. The entire tree depends on the roots and the earth for growth, strength, and stability. Science shows that rain formation depends on moisture, sunlight, and air. The list continues as we explore new ideas and expand our understanding of connections and relationships.

Networking is a powerful investment tool for success, and building relationships boosts your confidence by knowing you have a tribe to connect with for support and to offer support in return. Your ability to network is your currency, which you can trade for knowledge and ideas to grow yourself, your business, and your brand in the marketplace (the world). The power of networking can positively influence a person's life experience in several transformative ways, both personally and professionally.

Networking is one of the most powerful tools for both personal and professional growth. It goes beyond simply meeting people—it's about cultivating meaningful relationships that open doors to opportunities, insights, and growth you wouldn't find on your own.

- **ACTON: KEY AREAS WHERE NETWORKING MAKES A STRONG PERSONAL IMPACT**
  - ★ **Expanding Opportunities**

    Career Advancement: Networking helps you discover job openings or job leads, promotions, and collaborations that may never be publicly advertised.

    Business Growth: Entrepreneurs and professionals can find clients, investors, or partners through trusted connections.

    Mentorship: A strong network gives you access to mentors who can guide you in making smart decisions. Opens doors to opportunities through

    networking connects you to people who can offer partnerships, or referrals.

    Many roles and opportunities are filled through relationships rather than applications alone.

It can accelerate career growth or even pivot you into a new path entirely.

For instance, a casual conversation at an event could lead to a job interview or a mentorship opportunity.

★ **Gaining Knowledge and Insights**

Industry Trends: Engaging with peers and leaders keeps you informed on evolving practices, tools, and innovations in your field.

Problem-Solving: Networking allows you to learn from the experiences of others, offering fresh perspectives and solutions.

Skill Development: Conversations with others often expose you to new ideas, techniques, or training resources you might not find on your own. Improves Problem-Solving & Innovation

Collaborating with others allows you to crowdsource solutions to problems you're facing.

Shared knowledge and diverse perspectives can help you see challenges in a new light.

★ **Building Visibility and Credibility.**

Builds Confidence and Communication Skills.

Regular networking enhances your ability to present yourself and articulate your ideas.

You learn to engage with people from diverse backgrounds, which helps build emotional intelligence.

This confidence often spills over into other areas of life—public speaking, leadership, or personal relationships.

Personal Branding: Consistent networking strengthens your professional identity and helps others recognize your skills and values.

Reputation: When you contribute knowledge, support others, and show reliability, you build trust and credibility in your community.

Referrals: A respected network often becomes your best advocate, recommending you for roles, projects, or opportunities.

★ **Enhancing Confidence and Communication— Social Skills:**

Networking pushes you out of your comfort zone, helping you practice effective communication and active listening.

Self-Confidence: Positive interactions with diverse groups build your confidence to share ideas, pitch projects, or lead initiatives.

Cultural Competence: Connecting with people from different backgrounds broadens your perspective and adaptability.

★ **Personal Growth and Fulfillment.**

Support System: Networking creates communities where encouragement, accountability, and empathy flow both ways.

Inspiration: Meeting ambitious, resilient individuals can spark motivation and creativity in your own journey.

Friendships: Many professional connections grow into lasting personal relationships that enrich your life beyond work. It fosters personal growth..

Being around driven, curious, or like-minded individuals inspires self-reflection and ambition.

You gain exposure to new ideas, industries, and cultures, expanding your worldview.

For instance, talking to an entrepreneur might spark your interest in launching your own project.

★ **Networking with a Purpose.**

Learn from peers for connections and collaborations, mentors for clarity and opportunities, and diverse industries for innovation and increased knowledge. Endeavor to surround yourself with forward-thinking people inside and outside your field by joining professional associations or online communities to exchange ideas, collaborate on projects, and gain early insight into emerging trends.

Nugget: Cross-industry networking (e.g., tech + healthcare) often sparks the most innovative ideas.

★ **Strengthens Support Systems.**

Networking can provide emotional and professional support during life's challenges.

Having a network means you're not navigating transitions like job loss, relocation, or personal change alone. Improves building new relationships and connections. Networking fosters the building of new relationships with people from across the globe, thus enabling limitless collaboration and access to opportunities and a stronger support system.

★ **Creates Legacy and Influence.**

As your network grows, you gain opportunities to reciprocate service and love through mentorship, advocacy, or leadership. The growth of your network increases your influence as you have the privilege of working alongside others who may be even more influential and talented, giving you more access to even greater opportunities.

Helping others reinforces purpose and fulfillment in your own journey.

Networking thus enriches life by turning connections into catalysts for growth. It's not just who you know, it's who you grow with. Continue to seek areas where your contribution can benefit more effectively and make offers.

Learn to build others up in your home, community, and nation, for you never know whom you might help and need help from along the way. This is the best way to increase influence and build enduring wealth.

("And let us consider one another so as to incite(provoke) one another to love and good works," Hebrews 10:24 KJV.)

Networking is not just about "getting ahead"—it's about creating a two-way exchange of value. By nurturing authentic relationships, you set the foundation for sustained success, resilience, and fulfillment in both your personal and professional life.

CHAPTER EIGHT

❖ MASTER FINANCIAL INTELLIGENCE —WEALTH BUILDING

["But you shall remember the LORD your God, for it is He who gives you the strength (power) to gain wealth, so that He may establish His covenant, which He swore to your fathers, as it is this   day...Deut 8:18. RC]

["The silver is mine, and the gold is mine, saith the LORD of hosts. ". Haggai 2:8 KJV]

Wealth is not just income, it is what one receives, keeps, grows, and protects. Financial intelligence isn't just about knowing how to make money—it's also about learning how to manage, multiply, and sustain it. It's the skillset that turns income into long-term wealth and freedom.

Thriving in abundance in your life also involves making wise and prudent financial decisions. Financial literacy is the foundation for financial independence and effective wealth creation. Understanding money and wealth and their importance in life is essential for growth and prosperity in all areas. Mastering finances can greatly improve a person's life by providing freedom, confidence, and long-term security.

Knowing why you are building wealth is essentially valuable. Sometimes, people build wealth but don't know the reason why and that may be detrimental to the individual and their families. To build and sustain wealth, you need to understand your family history. Research the values and beliefs your family holds concerning wealth, the laid down plan or blueprint for creating, protecting and perpetuating wealth, and, more importantly, your family's covenant with God concerning wealth. Seek God through His word, and He will reveal things you do not know. A deeper exploration of how mastering finances improves a person's life—examining the psychological, social, professional, and generational impacts—is of essence in a person's life in this day and age.

["Call unto me, and I will answer thee, and show thee great and mighty things, which thou knowest not." Jer 33:3 KJV]

["For I know the plans I have for you," declares the Lord, "plans to prosper you and not to harm you, plans to give you hope and a future." Jer 29:11 KJ]

- STRATEGIC FINANCIAL INTELLIGENCE APPLICATIONS AND IMPACT

Learning money and understanding its application in your life, and making healthy financial decisions, may lead to your success in the following areas:

★ **Reduces Stress and Anxiety.**

Money management is one of the leading causes of stress in the world. When you have knowledge and control over your finances, knowing what's coming in, what's going out, and where it's going, you gain peace of mind and reduce financial-related anxiety, improving your overall mental and emotional well-being

★ **Financial Control Equals Peace of Mind.**

When people understand how to manage their finances well, budgeting, investing, saving, paying bills, and reducing debt, they relieve a major source of mental burden. Constant financial chaos leads to sleepless nights, anxiety over bills, and fear of unexpected expenses.

By contrast, financial mastery creates a sense of inner calm and peace, improving overall mental health and emotional resilience.

★ **Increases Freedom and Choices.**

Financial mastery allows you to choose where you live, travel when you want, invest in personal passions, and change careers without fear of instability.

Essentially, it gives you options, which is a powerful form of freedom. Freedom of choice.

★ **Money as a Tool, not a Trap.**

Having a poor money mindset makes you feel like making a lot of money is a trap. On the contrary, mastering finances as a tool, enables people to live by design, not by default. It opens doors to quitting toxic jobs and gives them the freedom to travel or take sabbaticals. They are able to pursue their passions, education, or purpose-driven work.

Without money stress, people are empowered to say yes to what aligns with their values and no to what doesn't. People are more likely to set boundaries that align with their values and foster trust.

★ **Enables Goal Achievement.**

From buying a home to starting a business or retiring early, wise financial planning helps turn dreams into achievable, actionable plans. Budgeting, saving, and investing are tools that convert intention into reality.

★ **More Resources, More Giving.**

Those who manage their money well can have a meaningful social impact by helping family or community members in need, supporting charities and nonprofits, and investing in social enterprises.

Financial mastery allows you to make a difference without compromising your own security.

★ **Improves Relationships.**

Financial strain often leads to conflict, especially in marriages or family life. Mastering money encourages transparency, teamwork, and trust, strengthening relationships and reducing conflict. Stronger Relationships

★ **Less Conflict, Encourages More Connection.**

Money disagreements are a top cause of personal and professional conflicts such as, marital tension and family disputes, disagreements in business relationships, etc. Financial literacy promotes transparent conversations, shared objectives, and planning, and better problem-solving in relationships, whether in the family, community, or business environment.

When everyone is on the same page, there's less blame and more teamwork, strengthening relationships across generations.

★ Builds and Perpetuates Generational Wealth.

Financial literacy empowers you to create a legacy. By saving, investing wisely, and avoiding debt traps, you position yourself to help your children, support causes you believe in, or start a business that lasts beyond your lifetime, thereby instilling your legacy of wealth building in your children and grandchildren. Thinking Beyond Survival and mastering money allows you to plan not just for today, but for the next generation. You can build generational wealth, teach your children financial literacy, and leave behind assets instead of debts. It shifts your mindset from surviving paycheck to paycheck to building a legacy and ensuring that there is continuity to perpetuate the wealth.

★ Boosts Confidence and Discipline.

Taking charge of your finances reinforces a mindset of responsibility and self-discipline. You begin to feel more capable in other areas of your life, too, because you're making intentional, well-informed choices. Personal growth and discipline reveal that money habits reflect life habits, which suggests that your personal growth is directly proportional to your money habits, which in turn reflect your life habits or choices. Budgeting, delayed gratification, and investing all require discipline. When you master your finances, you build goal-setting habits, long-term thinking, and self-control.

These qualities extend to other areas of life, such as health, time management, and decision-making.

★ **Prepares for Life's Uncertainties.**

Emergencies happen, such as job loss, medical bills, unexpected repairs, and a well-managed financial plan includes emergency savings and insurance, reducing your vulnerability to life's surprises. This provides long-term security and preparedness. Life is unpredictable, but finances don't have to be. Emergencies and curveballs are inevitable, but a financially prepared person has emergency savings, health, and life insurance backup plans for income loss.

This cushion provides security, allowing you (people) to face life's uncertainties with confidence instead of fear.

★ **Supports Personal and Professional Growth**

Whether it has to do with going back to school, that is, investing in yourself by enrolling and completing courses, certifications, and acquiring tools that elevate your career skills and expertise, taking a career risk, or investing in your health, financial security, it makes it easier to invest in yourself and your future. Career and business empowerment presents more opportunities and less desperation. When finances are stable, people can invest in career development, start a side hustle or business, wait for the right job, and not accept just any job.

Financial mastery provides you with the leverage and freedom to grow personally and professionally without compromising your integrity or settling due to desperation.

You can then diversify your income streams to create financial security. Avoiding unnecessary debt and making strategic investments in assets that appreciate over time.

★ **The True Power of Financial Mastery.**

Mastering your finances is not just about numbers. It's about quality of life. It's the foundation for peace of mind, freedom of choice, empowered relationships, personal fulfillment, and long-term impact on generations.

It's not about how much money you make, but how intentionally you manage and grow what you have.

★ Understanding Money Beyond Income

Difference between Assets and Liabilities: Assets put money in your pocket (investments, real estate, businesses), while liabilities take money out (debt, luxury items that don't grow in value).

Cash Flow Awareness: Track where your money comes from and where it goes. Wealth is built when you control and direct your cash flow intentionally.

★ Building a Wealth Mindset

Think Long-Term: Wealth creation is about planting seeds today for future harvests.

Abundance vs. Scarcity Thinking: Believing opportunities are abundant opens your mind to investment and growth.

Continuous Learning: Financial literacy evolves—commit to reading, networking, and learning from mentors.

★ Core Pillars of Financial Intelligence Budgeting & Discipline

Know how to live below your means without sacrificing growth.

Saving with Purpose: Save not just for emergencies, but also for investments.

Investing Wisely: Understand risk, return, and diversification (stocks, bonds, real estate, entrepreneurship).

Tax & Legal Knowledge: Knowing how to legally minimize taxes and protect assets is crucial for wealth preservation.

★ Creating Streams of Income.

Active Income: Your salary, wages, or business profits.

Passive Income: Dividends, rental income, royalties, or automated businesses.

Portfolio Income: Earnings from investments like stocks, bonds, or mutual funds.

Diversification ensures stability and resilience in wealth-building.

★ Protecting and Growing Wealth

Risk Management: Insurance, emergency funds, and legal structures safeguard your assets.

Smart Debt Use: Leverage debt for wealth-building (e.g., real estate investment), not consumption.

Compounding Power: Invest early and consistently; time magnifies returns

★ Legacy and Generational Wealth.

Estate Planning: Wills, trusts, and succession plans ensure your wealth benefits future generations.

Teaching Financial Literacy: Passing on knowledge is as important as passing on assets.

Philanthropy: Giving or chastity creates impact and strengthens your purpose beyond money.

Key Takeaway: Mastering financial intelligence equips you to not just earn, but to build lasting wealth. It's about balancing knowledge, discipline, and mindset so your money works for you—and for generations to come.

★ Professional Guide for wealth

Mastering Financial Intelligence: A Path to Wealth Creation

Key Takeaways:

  *Wealth is not just income—it's what you keep, grow, and protect.

  *A strong financial mindset opens doors to opportunities and stability.

  *Diversified income streams create resilience.

  *Protecting wealth is as important as creating it.

  *True wealth includes financial freedom, legacy, and impact.

  *Having a laid down blueprint for making wealth, keeping and growing wealth creates a pathway for perpetuating and protecting the wealth.

Action Steps:

  *Track your monthly cash flow.

  *Commit to saving and investing consistently.

  *Build at least one stream of passive income.

  *Learn tax and asset-protection basics.

  *Share financial knowledge with others.

This way, you'll increase your knowledge and understanding in wealth creation and financial literacy for personal and professional financial growth.

CHAPTER NINE

❖ **PRIORITIZE SELF-DISCIPLINE AND CONSISTENCY**

"This book of the law shall not depart out of thy mouth; but thou shalt meditate therein day and night, that thou mayest observe to do according to all that is written therein: for then thou shalt make thy way prosperous, and then thou shalt have good success." Joshua 1:8 KJV

In my journey through this life, I have learnt the true meaning of success and it isn't about occasional bursts of motivation, but it's about consistent and persistent actions. Consistency is considered the true foundation of trust and virtue, and often emphasizes the importance of persistent effort and unwavering dedication to achieving objectives and accomplishments and to building a solid stance for success. Consistency is the key to achieving and maintaining momentum. If you are persistent, you will get it, if you are consistent, you will keep it.

Optimizing self-discipline and consistency involves creating systems that support your life's objectives, habits, and mindset, even when motivation wanes. Start with a clear "why" with the knowledge that where purpose fuels discipline, discovery becomes inevitable.

- APPLICABLE TECHNIQUES FOR SELF-DISCIPLINE AND CONSISTENCY

★ Know why you want to be consistent, whether it's for your health, career success, financial freedom, or personal growth, and believing that it is possible to achieve it. A strong "why" gives meaning to your actions and sustains your drive during hard times. Guides you in setting clear objectives and breaking them down into daily actions. Build habits that support long-term success and help you stay disciplined even when results aren't immediate, with the awareness that compound effort leads to exponential returns.

★ Set Specific, Achievable objectives and work towards them

Clarity beats willpower. Break down big plans into small, manageable steps, and use SMART objectives techniques (Specific, Measurable, Achievable, Relevant, Time-bound), For instance, instead of saying "I want to get fit," say "I will walk for 30 minutes five days a week, that is a measurable and achievable objective!

★ Create Routines and Systems.

Habits are the backbone of discipline. Build daily routines that reduce decision fatigue. Use tools like planners, to-do lists, or habit trackers, and make your environment support your habits (e.g., remove unhealthy food, set out workout clothes the night before). In other words, be intentional with yourself and your habits and track your progress in real time because this is your real life.

★ Start Small and Build Momentum.

Small wins create big results. Begin with small, consistent actions, with the knowledge that success builds confidence and makes the habit stick. Focus on being consistent, not perfect. Progress over perfection always wins.

★ Track Progress and Celebrate Milestones.

Measure to motivate, use journals, apps, or charts to see your progress visually. Celebrate small wins, for it reinforces the behavior and keeps morale high.

★ Practice Self-Compassion.

Discipline yourself without shame. You will slip up sometimes, but don't quit, give yourself grace while staying firm on your objective. Most people quit because of self-condemnation and unforgiveness.

Talk to yourself like a coach, not a critic. Discipline thrives in a healthy mindset, not in guilt or harshness. For instance, say "you've got this, get back on track."

★ Limit Distractions and Triggers.

Protect your focus and identify what tempts you to break consistency, such as excessive social media scrolling, toxic people, clutter, and reduce those triggers. Create boundaries around time and energy (e.g., turn off notifications during work hours or during meetings, and personal time, such as meditation).

★ Build Accountability.

Acknowledge that external support strengthens internal resolve and share your goals with someone you trust. Be willing to accept feedback and work on your shortcomings; that is true accountability. Who are you accountable to in the season? Seek opportunities to be accountable.

You can also join a group, get a coach, or use an accountability app, because being seen and supported helps keep you motivated and consistent when willpower is low.

★ Visualize and Affirm Your Daily Visions.

Train your mind with discipline and commit to visualizing yourself succeeding by consciously seeing the action, feeling the outcome, and affirming the vision through the use of your words.

Use daily affirmations like: "I follow through on my commitments" or "I am disciplined and focused."

★ Rest, Reflect, and Realign.

Resting, reflection, and realignment are often overlooked, yet they are core pillars of sustainable success. Together, they refresh your mind, clarify your direction, and fine-tune your actions, sharpening your ability to focus and execute with excellence.

Rest Recharges Mental and Physical Energy. And here is why it matters: Mental fatigue reduces clarity, patience, and decision-making ability. Burnout decreases motivation and creativity, leading to poor execution.

Here's how rest helps: Sleep enhances memory, learning, and problem-solving abilities. Short breaks improve productivity and focus (e.g., Pomodoro technique). Downtime promotes emotional regulation and resilience.

"Rest is not a reward. It's a requirement."

Reflection Provides Insight and Clarity.

And here's why it matters: Without reflection, you're likely to repeat mistakes or waste effort on unproductive paths. It helps you assess what's working, what's not, and why.

How reflection helps: Encourages self-awareness and ensures growth. It also promotes intentional, not reactive, action and helps realign your time and effort with your deeper purpose and values.

Here are some suggested reflection questions to ask:

What did I achieve today?

What energized me this week?

What distracted me from my priorities?

What success inspired me, be it big or small?

Realignment Ensures Strategic Focus.

Here's why it matters: Life and priorities change, and without regular realignment, your actions can drift from your true objectives and purpose. Drifting leads to misalignment and misalignment leads to frustration and wasted energy.

Here's how realignment helps: It enables you to reset your focus toward your current objectives. It also refines your routine, priorities, and environment to support success better and reignites motivation by reconnecting you to your "why." Always ensure sustainability by avoiding burnout through a schedule of rest and recharge time.

In practice you can use these suggested principles:

Daily: Take short breaks, journal for 5-10 minutes, outline and adjust tomorrow's plan today. Always prepare for the next day ahead of time.

Weekly: Review wins/losses, set micro-objectives. In other words, short-term objectives are more effectively realized within the weekly cycle.

Monthly or Quarterly: Audit your habits, reset objectives, re-prioritize. Semi-long-term objectives are accomplished and accounted for better on a monthly or quarterly level.

Yearly: Bring all your activities into perspective, and evaluate them under a 'microscopic lens', ensuring that you are ending your year strong and beginning the new or next year boldly with precision, enthusiasm and expectation.

The Cycle: Rest → Reflect → Realign → Reignite

Phase	Outcome
Rest	Restores energy and sharpens focus
Reflect	Clarifies progress and obstacles
Realign	Refocuses effort and direction

This cycle keeps you from operating from unawareness, or on autopilot, and empowers you to execute with intention, energy, and precision.

Rest revives your energy, reflection increases your insight, and realignment restores your purpose, enabling you to reignite more congruently from within your spirit. Together, they create a powerful feedback loop that boosts your focus and sharpens your execution over time.

Employ the discipline formula.

"It's not about being perfect every day. It's about showing up consistently, forgiving yourself when you fall, and getting back on track every time." And regularly reflecting on what's working or not, and always realigning your habits with your objectives as life changes.

CHAPTER TEN

❖ ADAPT AND EVOLVE WITH THE WORLD AROUND YOU (MARKET TRENDS)

["..For we wrestle not against flesh and blood, but against principalities, against powers, against the rulers of the darkness of this world, against spiritual wickedness in high places." Eph 6:12. KJV]

Knowing what you're up against in the world of systems and algorithms, gives you an added advantage in devising your own path through it. Without the knowledge, there's a high probability of not achieving your desired outcome. In order for you to remain relevant and stay ahead of your contemporaries, you may need to stay informed about trends in the world, economic trends such as business opportunities and growth, technological innovations, and new ideas in industries such as agriculture, architecture and energy, as a person and also in your field of expertise for professional relevance.

Adapting to and growing with world trends, as well as within your field of expertise, requires continuous learning, strategic awareness, and flexible action. In today's fast-changing global landscape, it's not the strongest who thrive, but the most adaptable. It is of great importance that a person stays relevant, innovative, and ahead of the curve in all areas of their life.

Stay informed about market and industry trends with the understanding that knowledge is power, and timely information provides a competitive edge. You can achieve this by subscribing to industry journals, newsletters, and reputable global news outlets such as The New York Times, as well as following thought leaders and trend analysts on platforms like Threads, LinkedIn, YouTube, Facebook, or X (Twitter).

Endeavor to attend conferences, webinars, and trade shows, even virtually, within your area of expertise to identify upcoming shifts. For example: A data analyst monitors trends in AI automation, ethics, and data privacy.

A fashion designer observes how sustainability and fast fashion are transforming consumer behavior. You may also invest in continuous learning, recognizing that adaptation equals lifelong education. For instance, taking online courses, attending workshops, Masterminds, or pursuing certifications relevant to your field or even in a different field of interest. Additionally, learning complementary skills that broaden your expertise, such as a marketer learning data analytics or UX design, can enhance your confidence as a professional.

Adapting the use of microlearning—spending 5–10 minutes daily on new content or skills—can be beneficial.

"Those who stop learning become outdated faster than the technology itself." Unknown

Read industry news and reports regularly. Learn emerging technologies and skills that give you a competitive edge. Be flexible to pivot when necessary and embrace change.

- **PRACTICAL WAYS TO ADAPT AND TRANSFORM**

  ★ Practice Strategic Adaptability.

  Don't resist change, pilot it, and be willing to pivot when your old methods stop working. Try new tools, workflows, or platforms, even in small doses. Learn to analyze global events (e.g., pandemics, political shifts, tech booms) and ask: How might this affect my industry, and how can I respond proactively?

  ★ Leverage Data and Technology

  Use technology tools to make smarter decisions and understand how data shapes decisions in your field. Adopt relevant digital tools, whether it's AI, automation, analytics, or collaboration platforms. Use market intelligence platforms to monitor trends in real time (e.g., Google Trends, Statista, Gartner).

★ Innovate Within Your Role.

Be a change-maker, not just a follower, suggest improvements, lead initiatives, and propose new ideas, even if they're experimental. Stay curious and ask: What unmet need exists in my field? How can I solve it better or differently?

Think globally and consider how trends in other markets may influence your local context. Read and listen to international news on the global market economy.

★ Align Your Personal Brand with Relevant Value

Stay visible and relevant by   sharing what you're learning or building on LinkedIn or in industry groups. Update your résumé, portfolio, and skillset regularly to reflect market-relevant expertise. Position yourself as a forward-thinking contributor, not just a task-completer.

★ In summary: Adaptation = Awareness + Action + Agility

Element	Practice
Awareness	Stay informed and track trends
Action	Keep learning, testing, and networking
Agility	Pivot quickly and innovate boldly

["..Behold, I will do a new thing; now it shall spring forth; shall ye not know(perceive)it? I will even make a way in the wilderness, and rivers in the desert." Isaiah 43:19 KJV]

"The future doesn't belong to the most talented. It belongs to the most adaptable."

Therefore, adapt to engaging in meaningful conversations in which you don't just ask for help, but you also offer value in return. Stay active in communities, online and offline, where opportunities arise. And always believe in possibilities.

★ **Focus on Abundance, Not Scarcity**

A scarcity mindset keeps you stuck in fear, while an abundance mindset helps you see endless possibilities.

★Believe that opportunities are limitless, not scarce.

  ★ Celebrate others' successes instead of seeing them as competition.

  ★ Operate with gratitude and confidence, knowing that success is a matter of time, mindset and action.

CHAPTER ELEVEN

❖ BALANCE WORK WITH WELL BEING (HEALTH)

True success isn't just financial, it's also about health, relationships, and fulfillment of one's purpose. Health is a component of the wealth of Life. Health is one of the most foundational and irreplaceable components of the wealth of life. True wealth isn't measured solely in monetary or material possessions, but in the quality and richness of one's overall experience of life, and health is central to that experience.

Balancing work with health and well-being enhances a person's life by creating a foundation for sustained success, happiness, and resilience. It allows individuals to perform at their best without sacrificing their physical, emotional, or mental wellness.

Health, as a component of life's wealth, is the state of physical vitality, mental clarity, and emotional balance that enables a person to fully engage in and enjoy life's opportunities, responsibilities, and relationships. Health is considered true wealth because it protects time. Without health, time is often consumed by illness, limitations, or treatment, robbing people of life's joys.

You can rebuild your finances, replace a job, or recover from failures, but poor health, once deeply compromised, often limits every other aspect of life. In this way, health is not just a part of wealth, it is its foundation. Take care of your mental and physical health. Spend time with loved ones and nurture meaningful relationships. Pursue passions outside of work to maintain a well-rounded, abundant life.

- **PRACTICAL TECHNIQUES TO LIFE-WORK BALANCE**

★   Improves Productivity and Focus.

Good health enables productivity by providing the strength and energy necessary to pursue dreams, work effectively, and achieve objectives.

A healthy body supports a sharp mind through regular rest, movement, and good nutrition, which   improve brain function, memory, and attention. People who prioritize well-being often get more done in less time, with fewer mistakes.

" Rested minds make better decisions than overworked ones "

★   Strengthens Mental Health and Emotional Stability.

Well-being is the root of resilience. Chronic overwork leads to anxiety, burnout, and emotional fatigue. A well-balanced life supports mental well-being and emphasizes mental health as essential to decision-making, resilience, and emotional stability.

Prioritizing mental health through mindfulness, therapy, or downtime helps build emotional intelligence and self-regulation.

You're less reactive and more composed under pressure.

★   Enhances Long-Term Career Sustainability.

Avoid burnout   and build endurance. Careers arc marathons, not sprints. Ignoring health for short-term gains often leads to breakdowns later.

People who pace themselves are more likely to have longevity and more fulfilling careers.

★   Improves Relationships and Social Life.

Balance fuels connection. When you're not exhausted or distracted by work stress, you're more present with family, friends, and loved ones.

Healthy relationships are a major contributor to life satisfaction. When you're healthy, you're more present, engaged, and capable of nurturing meaningful connections.

★   Boosts Creativity and Innovation

Great ideas need space to breathe. Overworking dulls creativity. A healthy body's breaks and play stimulate the mind, helping you think more clearly and innovatively.

Activities like nature walks, reading, or hobbies often spark "aha" moments, whilst also strengthening your physical body, improving your overall health and wellbeing.

★   Promotes Physical Health.

Your body is your lifelong asset. Sitting too long, skipping sleep, or ignoring exercise weakens the immune system and increases the risk of chronic illness. Balanced routines that include movement, hydration, and sleep boost energy and reduce sick days. A healthy mind and body fuel longevity & quality of life. Health isn't just about living longer, it's about living better.

With better health and living, you are able to pass onto the next generation, nurturing them and infusing them with the energy, knowledge, and joy that sustain a generation, allowing it to continue the cycle of life.

★   Builds Self-Worth and Personal Fulfillment.

Life is more than a job title, material things, and money. Investing in yourself, through self-care, spiritual growth, or leisure, reinforces that your value isn't solely tied to output.

An improved self-worth leads to a deeper sense of purpose and identity.

★   Aligns With Holistic Success.

True success = Achievement + Wellness

You're not truly successful if you're succeeding at work but failing in health or happiness.

Balance ensures that your objectives are sustainable, meaningful, and rooted in whole-life fulfillment, not just external achievements. In this charismatic world, people place emphasis on external and superficial achievements, leaving behind their most significant asset, their health and well-being. *("For what shall it profit a man, if he shall gain the whole world, and lose his own soul?" Mark 8:36.) ("Beloved, I wish above all things that thou mayest prosper and be in health, even as thy soul prospereth." 3John 2. KJV)*

★   Balance Brings Wholeness

Benefit Area	*Impact of Work-Life-Health Balance*
Mental Focus	*Improves clarity, decision-making*
Physical Health	*Reduces illness, increases energy*
Emotional Resilience	*Lowers stress, prevents burnout*
Social Connection	*Strengthens relationships*
Creativity	*Sparks new ideas and innovation*
Self-Fulfillment	*Enhances life satisfaction*

"Balance isn't always about equality in time, it's about intentional priorities." Unknown

CHAPTER TWELVE

❖ TAKE BOLD ACTION —STARTING NOW

("Now faith is the substance of things hoped for, the evidence of things not seen." Heb 11:1 KJV)

The biggest difference between those who succeed and those who don't is action. Taking the first step even when you don't see the whole staircase, is faith. Stop waiting for the "perfect" moment. Start where you are with what you have. Take one bold step today, no matter how small, it compounds into major success. The biggest difference between taking action in the now versus delaying or hesitating is momentum; acting now creates it; waiting kills it.

- PRACTICAL REASONS WHY TAKING ACTION IN THE NOW MATTERS MOST:

★ Immediate Progress vs. Stagnation

Now: You make tangible steps, learn, adjust, and grow. Later: You stay stuck in analysis, fear, or procrastination. Procrastination is the enemy of progression

★ Confidence Builds vs. Doubt Grows.

Now: Action reinforces belief, even small wins build confidence.

Later: Inaction feeds self-doubt, and the longer you wait, the harder it becomes.

★ Doors Open vs. Opportunities Fade.

Now: Acting opens up unexpected opportunities and connections.

Later: Delayed decisions can result in missed chances or closed doors.

★ You Shape the Outcome vs. Circumstances.

Now: You're proactive, steering your life.

Later: Life happens to you, rather than because of you.

The bottom line is, taking action now is the difference between potential and progress. It transforms vision into reality. Even imperfect action beats perfect inaction. *Just believe. Just do it. * And since we have the same spirit of faith, according to what is written, "I believed and therefore I spoke," we also believe and therefore speak;"*

There comes a point in your journey where desire is no longer enough, intention is no longer enough, and dreaming is no longer enough.   Healing, transformation, and destiny all demand bold action. Bold action is not reckless. It is not impulsive. It is not driven by fear or desperation. Bold action is purpose in motion. It is the courage to move in alignment with who you are becoming — not who you used to be.   Bold Action Begins With Clarity and before you step forward with power, you must know what you are stepping toward. Clarity shapes your decisions. Clarity strengthens your resolve. Clarity silences confusion and cuts through distractions. When you know your desired outcome, your actions become intentional instead of random.

Bold action requires emotional courage and you cannot take bold steps while clinging to old fears. Bold action means risking comfort for growth, choosing faith over doubt, facing your insecurities, letting go of the familiar, refusing to shrink when life stretches you. Emotionally, it is the decision to honor your future more than your fear. Action transforms vision into reality and bold action is the bridge between where you are and where you want to be,
who you are and who you are destined to become, and the life you have and the life you desire to live.
Dreams remain dreams until movement gives them form. Vision without action is imagination and vision with action becomes manifestation.

Bold steps create momentum. The moment you take one courageous step, life responds and momentum begins. Doors open, resources appear, people align, and opportunities reveal themselves. Bold action also activates the energy of movement — and movement attracts miracles. Bold action requires responsibility. Boldness is not loud — it is accountable. It means taking ownership of your decisions, habits, patterns, boundaries, healing, and direction.

You cannot obtain a desired outcome through passivity. Results follow responsibility and bold action breaks cycles. It is a fact that cycles don't break through wishing. They break through courageous decisions. When you set boundaries — that's bold action.

When you walk away from dysfunction — that's bold action.

When you choose healing over history — that's bold action.

When you invest in your growth — that's bold action.

Each courageous move is an act of "*rebellion*" against the strongholds and patterns in your life that had held you back.

Boldness aligns you with destiny. Bold action is not just physical movement — it is also a spiritual agreement. It announces: "*I am ready for the life that belongs to me.*" When you take brave steps heaven responds, purpose activates, destiny aligns, blessings accelerate.

Bold action is the language of people who refuse to settle. Outcome follows the courage, and desired outcomes are attracted to brave decisions not perfect decisions — brave ones. Your future doesn't require you to know everything. It requires you to just start. Because when you move with boldness everything works together to help you fulfill purpose. You are able to affirm: " I am worthy of the outcome I desire and seek." " I am capable of creating and achieving the life I envisioned ."
" I will not wait for permission to become who I already am ."

CHAPTER THIRTEEN

❖ **EXECUTE : FINISHING STRONG AND FAITHFUL!**

["His master said to him, 'Well done, good and faithful servant. You have been faithful and trustworthy over a little, I will put you in charge of many things; share in the joy of your master.' Matthew 25:23 AMP]

Pursuing a life strategy and finishing strong and faithful in all areas—personal, professional, spiritual, financial, and relational—requires vision, discipline, adaptability, and a legacy-minded approach. It's not about perfection but about intentional growth, resilience, and aligning with your purpose over the long term.

(*"Where there is no vision [no revelation of God and His word], the people are unrestrained; But happy and blessed is he who keeps the law [of God].* Prov 29:18 AMP)

● *STRATEGIC EXECUTION OF FINISHING IN STRENGTH*

★ Define a Clear Life Vision.

Without vision, there's no direction.

Ask: What kind of life do I want to live? What values define me?

Write a personal mission statement that includes your spiritual, relational, financial, and professional aspirations.

Set long-term objectives with a 5, 10, 15, 20, or even 30-year perspective.

"When you know where you are going, every step has purpose." Unknown

(*"And the LORD answered me, and said, Write the vision, and make it plain upon tables, that he may run that readeth it. For the vision is yet for an appointed time, but at the end it shall speak, and not lie: though it tarry, wait for it; because it will surely come, it will not tarry." Habakkuk 2:2-3)*

★ Break the Vision into Core Pillars.

Think in life domains:

Faith and purpose (spiritual growth, values)

Family and relationships (love, community, connection)

Health and vitality (physical and mental well-being)

Wealth and legacy (financial literacy, wealth building, stewardship)

Career and impact (calling, contribution)

Each domain should have clear objectives, specific habits, and establish checkpoints.

★ Build Daily Execution Systems.

Systems are stronger than willpower. Create routines and rhythms aligned with your objectives.

Use tools like habit trackers, journals, or accountability partners.

Prioritize consistency over intensity; small daily steps move mountains.

Examples: A morning routine that includes prayer, exercise, and observation review.

A weekly financial review every Sunday evening.

Daily check-in on your most important relationship (spouse, kids, parents, siblings, friends), every Monday morning.

★ Practice "Ruthless" Focus.

Don't chase everything, master the essentials.

Say no to distractions that pull you from your path and build boundaries to check yourself and others.

Focus on high-impact actions that move the needle in favor of your life domains and build you up.

Use tools like time blocking and prioritization (Eisenhower Matrix, 80/20 Rule).

★   Adapt with Wisdom and Humility.

Life changes, so should your strategy, and be open to pivoting.

Adjust your goals as seasons change accordingly (career shifts, health issues, family needs).

Reflect regularly: What's working? What's draining me? Where is my life out of balance? What improvement technique should I adopt?

Consistently have that internal dialogue, it's healthy for your mind and spirit. Learn to recognize your inner voice and listen, it has so much to whisper.

"Staying rigid in a changing world is not discipline, it's self-sabotage "

★ Surround Yourself with Purpose-Driven People.

Iron sharpens iron. Build a circle of wise, motivated, and honest counsel (individuals) who challenge and support you.

Learn from mentors, join masterminds, or faith-based communities.

Avoid isolation. It leads to drifting away. That notwithstanding, avoid surrounding yourself with sycophants and "yes men", that is the fastest way to self-destruction.

★ Measure Progress and Celebrate Milestones

Success leaves a signature(signs), look out for it. Schedule personal "strategy reviews" monthly, quarterly, and annually.

Celebrate victories, even the smallest ones, to build momentum and foster gratitude.

Track not just what you do, but who you're becoming.

★ Leave a Legacy—Finish Faithful.

Think beyond your lifetime. Considering the following: What impact will your life have when you're gone?

Finish strong by living every day with the end in mind. Making intentional decisions that benefit not just your generation but the next generations.

Pass on wisdom, faith, wealth, and love, not just the physical achievements. That is true generational wealth and building it may begin with you. Consider the possibility.

★ Perpetuate the Wealth

Ensure that the wealth you have created is perpetuated through built up principles, systems, patterns and structures. You must have the human structure well-built to ensure continuity of life and wealth. A well laid out plan, a blueprint for keeping the system running with or without you, to ensure continuity even centuries after you're gone.

★ Consider carefully these Key questions:

Who will benefit from how I lived?

What story will my life tell?

What am I building that lasts?

Do I have a designated survivor?

Do I have the human structure to ensure that my legacy passes on to generations successfully and efficiently?

These considerations are directed towards effectively and efficiently choosing your successor, one who has the kind of life, discipline, capacity and character to receive the weight and responsibility of the wealth and continue the legacy you have built with your very life.

The Life Execution Framework

Principle	Practice
Vision	Define life purpose and objectives
Structure	Break down into domains and build routines
Consistency	Execute small daily actions aligned with your mission
Adaptability	Pivot with grace as life shifts
Accountability	Stay connected to supportive, purpose-driven people
Reflection	Regularly review, refine, and renew your focus
	LegacyLive every day like it matters—because it does. Always begin with the end in mind.
Legacy	Live every day like it matters—because it does. Always begin with the end in mind.

"Success is not just finishing first, it's finishing faithfull.   "

CHAPTER FOURTEEN

❖ CONSIDERATIONS: FINAL THOUGHTS

[*"And he shewed me a pure river of water of life, clear as crystal, proceeding out of the throne of God and of the Lamb. In the midst of the street of it, and on either side of the river, was there the tree of life, which bare twelve manner of fruits, and yielded her fruit every month: and the leaves of the tree were for the healing of the nations."* Rev 22:1-2 KJV]

A life rising, even in chaos, always begins with optimism. Shifting the odds in your favor isn't about luck or external circumstances. It's about faith, mindset, willpower, clarity, strategy, precision, relentless execution and most importantly, the hand of God. When you start seeing challenges as opportunities, take calculated risks, and consistently level up your skills and mindset, you set yourself up to succeed and thrive in abundance, not just survive.

My journey through seasons of deep challenges, uncertainty, and soul-searching led me to stumble upon this path of possibilities and peace which was also borne out of grace; the grace that met me in my darkest moments and began to piece me back together and led me up to the light. Through that process as I was revived, I also discovered something life-altering: even in the midst of chaos, life still rises. Everything is possible. Liberation is possible. Peace is possible. And so is joy—not the surface kind, but the kind rooted deep in truth, perspective and love.

I believe that this communication, an invitation to reflect, to reconnect with your inner strength, and to remember what is still possible has caused you to rethink possibilities. You might not have found perfection here, but you surely found honesty. You might not have found all the answers, but you surely found direction. And most of all, you found hope -woven through every lesson, every struggle, and every breakthrough.

Success is within your reach. The question is: Are you ready to "work it and keep it"? (claim and receive)

["Therefore I will divide Him a portion with the great, And He shall divide the spoil with the strong, Because He poured out His soul unto death, And He was numbered with the transgressors, And He bore the sin of many, And made intercession for the transgressors." Isaiah 53:12. NKJV]

["And he shall be like a tree planted by the rivers of water, that bringeth forth his fruit in his season; his leaf also shall not wither; and whatsoever he doeth shall prosper." Psalm 1:3 KJV]

["My mouth shall speak the praise of the LORD; and let all flesh bless His holy name for ever and ever." Psa 145 : 21 KJV]

["For a righteous man may fall seven times, And rise again,..." Psa 24 : 16 NKJV]

www.ingramcontent.com/pod-product-compliance
Lightning Source LLC
Chambersburg PA
CBHW051552120626
46551CB00013B/1484